Panzerkampfwagen 35R 731(f) (Renault R35)

Origins of the Renault R35 3

1940 AFV Situation 19

Losses 22

French tanks Captured 24

Panzerkampfwagen 35R 731(f) (Renault R35) types 26

French Vehicles in Normandy 1944 26

Panzerkampfwagen 35R 731(f) (Renault R35) 30

Befehlspanzer 35R (f) (26 produced) 39

Munitionspanzer 35R 731(f) 41

Bergeschlepper 35R 731(f) (towing of vehicles) 43

Zugkraftwagen 35R 731(f) 43

4.7cm Pak(t) auf PzKpfw 35R (f) (200 produced) 46

5cm Pak38 auf PzKpfw 35R (f) 61

Flammenwerferpanzer 35R (f) 62

Mörserzugmittel 35R (f) (Artillerie-Schlepper) 64

Modifications 68

End of the line 71

Appendix 72

Literature 73

Origins of the Renault R35

In 1933, France was still searching for a good replacement for its FT17, that are clearly obsolete and at the end of their life.

The NC28 tank was just a modernized FT with a defective suspension. The D1 (poorly armoured) and D2 (too heavy) from
the 1924 program was not suited to the needs of the Infantry,
ie. close support of the foot soldiers.

The manufacturers usually waited for the GHQ to formulate what it wanted, but for once it is Hotchkiss that senses the need for a new light tank and prepares a project. This study is seen as promising enough for the 'Conseil consultatif de l'armement' (Armament Advisory Council) to draft a new program in August 1933 and an invitation to bid.

Renault R-35 as a light escort tank designed before World War II to replace the obsolete FT-17

The manufacturers was asked to work along these specifications:

Armament: 2MG or a small calibre gun Armour of 30 mm on vertical surfaces
Maximum weight of 6 metric tonnes

A 2-man crew
Average speed of 8 to 10 km/h

(the armour basis will be thickened to 40 mm in June 1934 after trials with the 25 mm SA34 antitank gun)

It is evident when reading the specifications that the new tank was plainly an updated Renault FT. The Infantry saw no point in high speed, as the tank should accompany the infantry and not wander away or outrun the troops in battle. The armament was meant to neutralize the enemy strong points, and antitank capabilities was not envisioned. The concept was still the one prevalent during WW 1 when the Kaiser's tanks were few and tank battles a rarity. Even when it was decided to give the light tanks a short 37mm SA18 gun, the supply of AP shells was low. A real antitank capability would only be obtained with the long barrelled 37 mm SA 37. The choice of a 2- man crew was based on several factors. The 1930 decade saw a low in the curve of birth rates in France after the bloodbath of the Great War, and a lack of personnel was feared. Futher more, the concept of the 'armoured infantryman' was still alive at this point with its wave tactic meant to overwhelm the enemy defences. So it is better to have 1,000 2-man tanks than 700 3-man ones. Last, the production costs are directly related to the size of the new AFV, and a 2-man tank is smaller than a 3-man one (also meaning lesser needs of armour quality steel; and material is always in short supply). This is no small factor in these days of financial crisis with limited funding for the military.

A total of 14 manufacturers submit a pre-project, whose 7 are retained in 1934. But only 4 constructors are contracted for prototypes for financial reasons, as there are already 3 'in the pipe' by Hotchkiss and one by the Atelier de Construction de Puteaux (APX). They are: Delaunay Belleville, FCM Batignolles Châtillon and Renault. The last one has been caught unaware by the quick start of Hotchkiss but it succeeds in being the first to complete its prototype because it begins assembly while the pre-projects are still under study. Both Delaunay Belleville and Batignolles Châtillon offerings are quickly dropped and only the ones designed by FCM and Hotchkiss will be pursued and see operational use.

The Renault's will to catch up with its competitors would have adverse side effects when the specifications where modified, because its prototype (called ZM under Renaults own nomenclature) was too advanced to take into account the increased armour basis. Only the turret can be armoured to 40 mm during the trials before the 'Commission d'expérimentation" on 20 December 1934. Renault was much in difficulty to keep within the weight limit because of the new armour thickness and also because it did not really master the casting process (a rather novel technique at the time). Casting large pieces of armour quality steel is a much advanced art that only the French industry can be said somehow to control, but the process has some weaknesses that the June 1937 trials will disclose. Out of twenty two 25mm shells fired from 0 to 1,000 m away with varying angles, 13 pierced the armour. Among the eighteen 37mm shells fired, 14 manage to do the same. The 8mm AP rounds perforate 5 or 6 times more than against laminated armour. But it was too late in 1937 to disturb production lines of much needed tanks... Back to the Renault prototype which now weighs 1.5 metric tons more than the specifications with its 2 MG turret. It undergoes several test phases with periods in the factory for modifications from January to

April 1935. The workshop delivers on 18 April 1934 the new APX R turret with the short 37mm SA18 gun and a Reibel 7.5mm MG. The gun is the one used on the FT 17, a reasoned choice. The weapon itself is proven and many FTs will soon be scrapped. Recycling their gun is an economy of time and money, as the design of any new gun is both long and a tricky thing. Last, the ammunition is already stockpiled in huge numbers.

37mm SA18 gun

The off-road performances of the prototype was rather bad as the weight distribution was uneven. Solutions to rectify this was searched as late as 1940. Another handicap was the trench crossing capability is seen as insufficient, but a temporary solution is found with the use of a tail adding 0.20 m to its capacity. It also prevents the tank to overturn when crossing a trench. The AMX tail is preferred to the Renault one in 1938 because it is both lighter and does not prevent the use of the rear tow shackles. Most of the tanks already produced could not be equipped with them before the Battle for France.

Despite all these questions still pending, and after a last series of trials, the Commission gives a green light if some modifications are implemented. The new tank is adopted as the char léger modèle 1935 R », model 1935R light tank. The international situation moves fast and a first order for 300 exemplars is signed on 29 April 1935. Several more follow to bring the total ordered in September 1939 to 1,800 plus 500 more for the war program. The delivered tanks amounted to 1,070 tanks in September 1939 and it can safely be estimated that more than 300 others were built up to June 1940, taking into account the 'built for export' models and the R40s.

Renault 35R showing its AMX tail for improved Trench crossing. The picture is from 7. SS-Freiwilligen-Gebirgs-Division „Prinz Eugen". The 7th SS Volunteer Mountain Division "Prinz Eugen" was a division of the Waffen SS, which was mainly set up in the northern Serbian Banat from ethnic Germans. She is best known for her war crimes in the partisan war(Bandenbekämpfung) in Yugoslavia. As a result, it shaped the historical picture of the war of the German Wehrmacht and Waffen-SS in Yugoslavia.

Trials & tests

The rather weak French offensive against Saarland in September 1939 demonstrated the large use of minefields by the Germans. The GHQ now measured the danger and called for mine clearing vehicles. From 2 to 5 April 1940, comparative trials were organized by the corresponding Commission of the Engineers against the 4 proposed devices.

The droppable rollers made by Captain Picard: the mines explode when struck by the rollers pulled by a long pole poin- ting to the front.

The striking weights of Captain Schwob: 2 groups of 4 tumbling devices pulled in front of the tracks, plus 4 more to the rear of the tank to sweep a 60 cm path along the axle of the tank.

The multi disk roller of Mr Corbier (working for AMX): three 1 m disks mounted on a common axle 1.2m wide.

The plough device by 'Ateliers de la Rhonelle' (working for AMX): the depth can be adapted and the mines are unearthed and set aside.

All these devices are tested on R35 chassis on various terrains and against French made mines mimicking the German Tellermines (but without explosives). The Picard and Schwob systems quickly prove unequal to the task as many mines manage to explode under the tank tracks. The plough gave good results on even ground but far worse on varied terrain.
The AMX antimines device SY4 clearly outperformed its opponents even though the tank is restricted to first gear becau- se of the added weight. Time runs out and 130 are immedia- tely ordered, but too late to get any delivered before the Armistice. The idea was not lost though as the plans was sent to the USA in June 1940 and the system was later mounted on mine clearing Shermans. France also tried it post-war on the B1 bis.

Several units tested fascine carrier devices at the end of 1939 or beginning of 1940. The R35 was not good off-road and the idea was to lay fascines to fill in shell holes or trenches, etc.

French R35 testing in mud, with what looks to be a Citroen-Kegresse half-track in the foreground

France

After the mobilization in September 1939, a new organization is adopted for the tank units. The RCC (Régiment de Chars de Combat/Battle Tank Regiments) are turned into mobilization centres and their former components into BCC (Bataillon de Chars de Combat/Battle Tank Battalions). There are 21 BCC equipped with Renault R 35s in France.
The total of delivered tanks on 2 September 1939 is 975 exemplars, 765 in France plus 49 in schools, 33 in depots and 45 stationed overseas (the exported tanks are not included). The grand total can be estimated to be more than 1,600). Each BCC fields 45 tanks in 3 companies of 4 troops (each 3 tanks) plus a support company of 5 tanks and a command tank. Each company commander rides in an additional tank. The battalion also uses around 100 vehicles and so is quite self-supporting: light off-road command vehicle (VLTT de commandement), supply tractor (Tracteur de ravitaillement

TRC Renault or Lorraine), recovery half-track (semi chenillé de dépannage Somua MCG 4), liaison and transport vehicles, field kitchens, etc...

Most of the BCCs are directly subordinated to the Infantry and are not part of divisions. The light tanks are only to play the part they were designed for, supporting the foot soldiers. More, the Infantry Directorate does not believe in large mechanized units, fearing the AFV'S will gain independence. If it has finally agreed to the creation of the DCR, it keeps a tight rein on most of the light tank battalions. The BCCs will end largely scattered on the whole front, literally detailed among the different army corps. No regrouping and coherent manoeuvring is possible then. The famous sentence heard during the biased Riom trial in 1941 (officially to search for the responsibilities after the Fall of France) takes its full meaning in that case: « We had 1,000 units of 3 tanks when the Germans had 3 units of 1,000... ».

It is impossible to relate the story of all these BCCs here. From Saarland to the bridges on the Loire River, the reports are unfortunately too similar. The tanks fighting in small numbers face a much more numerous opponent with the support of ubiquitous airplanes. But when involved in combined operations such as the one fought by the 4ème DCR in the attack to clear the Abbeville bridgehead, they did well without faltering.

They were many exploits during this campaign and the small R 35s often did wonders. The 40 mm armour proved imper- vious to the 37 mm shells over 300 metres. But the R35 was not designed to fight the Blitzkrieg war it had to face and the mechanic was often pushed to its limits with dire consequences. In the end, the tank revealed itself as correctly armoured and robust, but was that sufficient to obviate the bad off-road capacities and still to weak armament with no antitank capability?

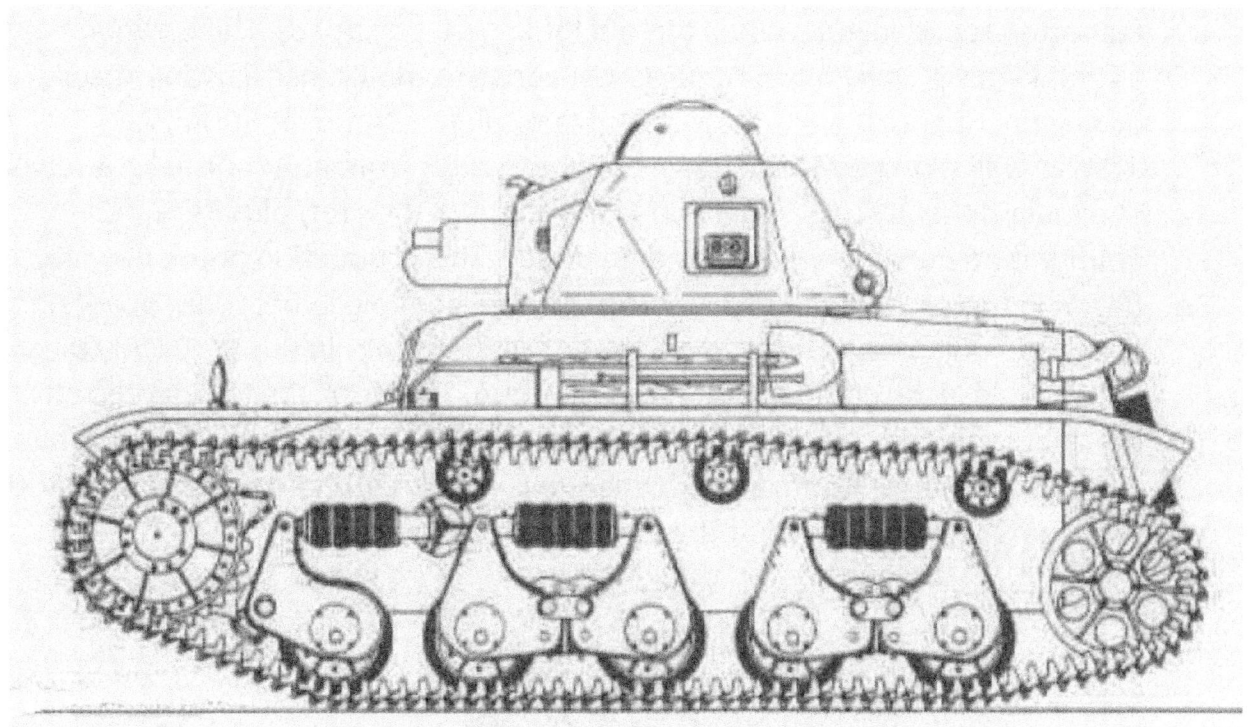

The whole concept of a 2-man crew tank was a handicap. The tank commander seated on a leather strap. He was tasked to observe, direct the tank and man the weapons. The observation cupola was free wheeling and he turned it with his helmet. He gave orders to his crew member by coded strokes on the driver's shoulders, as the engine was deafening anyway. When the tank commander was also the troop commander and worse still the battalion commander, he could only communicate with the other tanks in his outfit by coded flag movements through a special opening in the cupola. Closed down in the tanks, the crew was quite blind and deaf and could not really understand the developing situa- tion. It could only follow the instructions received before the fight and reach for the objective, whatever the outcome of the battle.

The 37 mm SA 38 gun

The 37 mm SA 18 gun was useless against the medium tanks as it could only pierce 15mm of armour plate at 1,000m. As the French light tanks had no designed antitank capacity (planned only for battle tanks) they where equipped with the same gun previously adopted on the FT17 (they were in fact often recycled guns when the old tanks was scrapped). The German antitank gun 3.7cm Pak 36 came as a surprise to the French liaison officers during the Spanish Civil War, as it is able to pierce 34mm at 600m. An answer was searched through a new 'powerful' 37mm gun for the light tanks. The main difficulty is to shoehorn it into the APX R turret, plus its larger ammunition boxes in an already tight space. The production of the new gun began in the second half of 1939 and they are sent piecemeal for conversion to the existing units, to a ratio of one out of four tanks in the BCC. Only the R40s would all be equipped with the new gun. The program to re-equip all the light tanks was scheduled to end in late 1940. The longer barreled gun was able to pierce 30mm at 1,000m. A reasonably estimate is more than 800 exemplars were delivered at the end of May 1940.

Polish Renault R35

Renault R40

Renault R40 from 48BCC

The main weakness of the Renault R35 lies with its suspension. The rubber treads disintegrate at a fast rate and the bogie layout lead to an uneven weight distribution. The result was a bad off-road capacity on wet soil and too much track 'sinking'.

Here an example of a French vehicle stuck in the mud

Several constructors offer a solution as it is both envisioned to equip the new tanks after the 1,500 mark, but also to modify the older tanks. The Lorraine firm logically based its product on its Lorraine 37 'chenillette', but this added too much weight (1.5 metric tonne) and it meant to to drill 118 new holes in the hull, all in exchange of no real benefit for the cross-country ride. The suspension presented by AMX had a strong resemblance to the D2 one with its vertical springing. It addressed many of the weight distribution problems. The track was a "Holt" type, looking much as a B tanks variant. The suspension housed 12 double wheels and the was protected from small projectiles and mud deposits by three vertical 8mm thick plates. The full weight increased 1.1 metric tonne.

For its part, Renault perfectly knew the limitations of its suspension and offered 3 solutions.

The first called for doubling the number of wheels (5 to 10) with the same type of horizontal springing but the end results was worse than on the original. The second solution used 9 wheels with a vertical suspension, much the same as AMX but with inferior performances. It was nevertheless envisioned at first to retrofit it to the existing tanks because it is easy to mount even in Regimental workshops. But the added weight was 2 metric tonnes and industrial reasons ultimately prevail as

Renault was to deliver the AMX suspensions. The last solution was to move back the idler to add a 6th wheel in front of identical to the front first but mounted opposite; the added weight was 700 kg. Comparative tests where made against this modification, the AMX offering and an unmodified Renault from 19 May 1938. AMX was the clear winner regarding slopes, obstacle crossing and overall stability plus track grip. But the speed did not improve and range was decreased because of the added weight. A third trial series was made before the Commission declared AMX the winner on 16 February 1939. Delivery of the "char léger modèle 1935 R modifié 1939" (usually known as the R40) was set for the 1,500th exemplar, ie. in February 1940. But the modifications of the production lines took longer to implement than foreseen so it is probable some forty more regular R35s were made because of the one month delay.

Captured Panzer 35R, kenn-nummer 731(f)

The exact number of delivered R40s is not known for sure, but can be realistically estimated to be ranging from 120 to 140. As always, the hectic events of June prevents establishing facts on these matters. The last R40s sent to the 'entrepôt général de Gien' (main depot of Gien) on 15 June 1940 are registered up to 51649, but it has been reported that the Renault factory in Saint Etienne (probably only an ad hoc assembly line) turned out tanks up to 51658.

Captured Renault R 40

The R40 in combat

The 40 and 48ème BCC where to form the 'demi brigade légère' (light half brigade) of the 4ème division cuirassée de réserve DCR (reserve armoured division). They where created on 16 November 1939 and are each outfitted with 33 FT17s and 3 H39s for training.

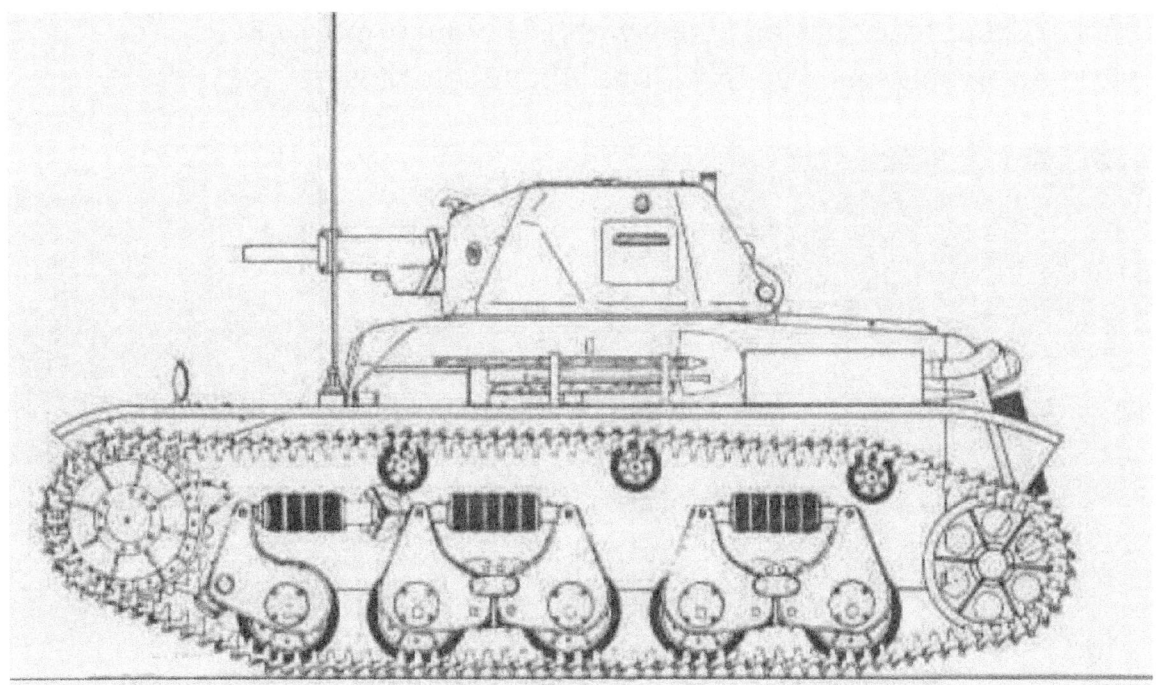

The 40ème BCC received 15 R35s and 30 R40s on 19 May 1940 in Versailles (near Paris) and was attached to 2ème DCR on 22 May. It launched a series of counter attacks and skirmishes against the German bridgehead at Corbie up to 31 May. 9 R35s was lost on the first day, the R40s fared better against the 37mm Pak guns, only the vision devices

being destroyed on several tanks. The battalion was transferred on the Bresle River where it would be involved in bitter rear-guard actions. On 10 June, the battalion was based near the Capital but began to move south on the 16. The withdrawal south of the Loire River was made difficult by incessant German probes, and several blocking positions was successfully established, they could only be temporary held. On 18 June, the unit still fielded 27 tanks and retreated while fighting up to the Armistice on 25 June, losing some more tanks (at least 4 scuttled).

The 48ème BCC was stationed at Toussus le Noble (near Versailles), and received its tanks from 19 to 22 May (16 R35s and 29 R40s). Attached to the 2ème DCR, the battalion was involved on 4 June in the Abbeville bridgehead battle. The tanks faced a tough resistance, unaware of the minefields and antitank guns. The 3 companies suffered heavy losses (11 destroyed and another lost in a ditch) and the attack failed. From 5 June, the unit took part with 2ème DCR in the covering force for the 7th Army Corps. The battles where furious especially on 8 June with 26 fit tanks (mainly R40s). The withdrawal gains speed up to 25 June when the unit is

Renault R40 before delivery

1940 AFV Situation

On 10th May 1940, Germany had 2636 tanks, 99 Panzerjäger I, 24 Sturmgeschütze, 38 15cm s.I.G.33 auf Pz.Kpfw.I, 6 8.8cm FlaK (Sfl) auf Sd.Kfz. 8 and at least 917 armored cars for a total of 3720 AFVs. 965 tanks was armed with a 3.7cm or 7.5cm gun, 99 Panzerjäger I with a 4.7cm gun and 24 StuG III with a 7.5cm gun. That leads to 1088 German AFVs armed with a good Anti Tank capacity (not counting the 6 8.8cm self-propelled AT guns).

On 10th May there was 2352 modern French tanks (2822 tanks with the obsolete FT17 and FCM-2C tanks) and about 609 armored cars or light reconnaissance tanks (330 armored cars and 279 light tanks). That makes 3101 French tanks (if the 279 AMR33/35s are counted as tanks) :
· only about 480 French tanks armed with a 47mm SA35 (including the B1bis tanks with their 75mm hull gun)
· about 350 which had the 37mm SA38 gun.
· from the about 279 AMR33/35s, 259 are only armed with a single 7.5mm or 13.2mm MG and 20 AMR35 had a 25mm SA35 gun (AMR35 ZT2 and ZT3). That makes 850 French tanks (27%) with an excellent to good anti-tank capacity.

The huge majority of the French tanks (2251 tanks) where light tanks armed with the 37mm SA18 gun or only MGs. The 37mm SA18 gun could be used at 300-400m against the Panzer I and Panzer II but to knock out a Panzer III Ausf.E/F (the previous models where less armored and easier to destroy) or a Panzer IV Ausf.C/D, they had to get as close as < 25-100m, whereas the enemy could destroy them at about 300m (3.7cm KwK) to 500m (7.5cm KwK) and even from longer range if you consider the obsolete Renault FT17.

On 10th May 1940, the British armored units had only 23 tanks with an AT capacity (Matilda II) and the Belgian armored units add 50 light tanks and 228 tank destroyers for a total of 1109 allied AFVs with a good to very good Anti Tank capacity.

But note that the German AFVs have an armor of 13-30mm (except the StuG III) whereas the French tanks (except the obsolete ones) have generally 40-60mm armor (35mm for the hull of the Hotchkiss H35).

There are comparable numbers of allied and German tanks with about 3000 tanks. If all the AFVs are counted there are 4112 allied vs 3720 German AFVs, with the obsolete French FT17 and FCM-2C tanks being counted (3642 allied vs 3720 German AFVs without them). This apparent "equality" in the number of tanks is purely mathematical and just taken as such by many people. The facts it is completely false.

All the about 3000 German tanks are concentrated in the 10 Panzerdivisionen unlike only about 960 French tanks in the DCR/DLM. Each DCR/DLM has less tanks than a Panzerdivision : there are roughly 10x300 German tanks against 6x160 French tanks and many dispersed battalions. That was the reality on the battlefield. The British 1st AD, which arrives during May 1940, concentrated the cruiser tanks but did not really change the balance and was quickly neutralized. All the Belgian tanks were dispersed in small numbers in their infantry divisions, the highest number of Belgian tanks could be found in the 1e division de chasseurs ardennais with about 50 AFVs. During the battle the Belgian AFVs were generally dispersed in groups of 2-4 AFVs.

In the DLM/DCR 80-90 tanks are only light tanks unlike what was initially planned (only medium/heavy tanks). 80% of these light tanks are armed with the 37mm SA18 L/21 gun and only 20% with the 37mm SA38 L/33 gun. The 37mm SA18 is only adapted to infantry support. A tank armed with the 37mm SA18 gun can actually destroy armored cars, Panzer I and Panzer II tanks at 300-400m but has to go closer than 25-100m to have a chance to destroy a Panzer III or Panzer IV, whereas it can itself be destroyed at 300-400m by them.

The DLMs were led by the cavalry corps HQ and the different DCRs were commanded by an armored group HQ. Nevertheless, these HQs had insufficient means unlike the Panzerkorps which had fully operational HQs.

Thanks to more radio sets the German tanks were able to better coordinate and concentrate their attack, changing more easily the attack axis. The French tanks favored better armor (and armament if we exclude the 37mm SA18 gun) rather than communications and speed. This better tactical regulation resulted in much more concentrated German armor against allied tanks, usually 4 vs 1, sometimes even 8-10 vs 1 odds.

The so-called German "superiority" was mainly due to :
· better high command and strategy, all the structural evolutions between Fall Weiss and Fall Gelb
· the organization of the Panzerwaffe concentrating all the tanks in the 10 Panzerdivisionen
· better inter-arms cooperation
· better tactical regulation, much more concentrated armor (usually 4 vs 1, sometimes 8-10 vs 1 odds)
· generally higher speed and mobility of the German tanks
· tracer and smoke shells available in the German tanks (not in the French ones)
· more radio sets allowing to better organize and control the maneuvers
· mostly always presence of observation planes (Hs126 and Fi156) to provide information about the allied position and direct artillery and aerial support
· mostly omnipresent close air support
· German tanks were spreading into the allied rears ... leading to issues to preserve a HQ or a fuel supply dump ... leading to tanks being abandoned and scuttled due to lack of fuel
· better and faster logistics in the armored units (and far less hindered by aerial attacks)
· 1-man turret in most of the French tanks and several very recently constituted units lacking training
· usually German tanks avoided combat with the heavy allied tanks like the Renault B1bis which constituted a big threat, they were rather engaged by 8.8cm FlaK, 10.5cm LeFH or aircrafts ... again inter-arms cooperation

Losses

If we list all the AFVs (tanks, tank-destroyers, self-propelled guns and armored cars) we can say that on 10th May 1940 about 4,112 Allied AFVs are facing about 3,720 German AFVs.

1) We can say that on 10th May 1940 the French army had a total 3,101 tanks in combat units. If we take into account the replacement of May-June 1940 (about 688 tanks) and the territorial/regional units (not counted among 'combat units' in my previous listing) actually engaging obsolete Renault FT17 tanks against the enemy we reach a figure of about 4,000 French tanks used during the whole 1940 campaign.

Concerning the French tanks lost during May-June 1940 :
According to "Survey of Allied tank casualties in World War II" (Alvin D. Coox and L. Van Loan Naisawald) - Operations Research Office, Johns Hopkins University, Fort Lesley J. McNair (1951) based on data provided by the SHAT (Service Historique de l'Armée) : "Notice relative aux destructions d'engins blindés au cours de la guerre 1939-1945" and "Fiche : Annexe à l'étude sur les pertes en chars au cours de la campagne 1939-1940 (SECRET), received by Office of the Army Attache, American Ambassy in Pairs, in reply to an Operations Research Office request of 4th August 1950.

The following data represent the losses of the tank battalions, the DCRs, the DLCs, the DLMs, the reconnaissance groups and the territorial units. Tanks hit but salvaged and repaired by the field echelons in a very short time were screened out. Tank losses for the indicated period of time by number and percentage were as follows :
FRENCH TANK CASUALTY DATA BY CAUSE, 1939-1940
· Artillery (field guns, PaK, FlaK and tanks) : 1,669 (95.4%)
· Mines : 45 (2.6%)
· Aircrafts : 35 (2.0%)
--> TOTAL : 1749 tanks (including 151 obsolete tanks - Renault FT17 tanks)
There were also tanks which were abandoned, scuttled or set afire by their crews to avoid captured. [Personal note : the total number including breakdowns/damages and then abandoned tanks is probably closer to 2,000 French tanks].

No data exists as to those tanks repaired in factories and parks between 10th May and 25th June 1940, or those salvaged on the battlefield, repaired and sent back into battle.

The same document states that from 10th May to 25th June 4,071 tanks of all types were actually engaged and 3,413 of them were modern tanks.

It is striking that even with huge air superiority and omnipresent close air support only 35 French tanks were taken out by German aircraft's. Several French tanks were destroyed by AT mines, implying a French attack like in

Montcornet or Abbeville. It would have been interesting (but impossible) to know how many of the 1,669 tanks taken out by artillery have been actually destroyed by German tanks and not by AA / AT / field guns (or a combination of several means) [e.g. roughly all the Renault B1bis heavy tanks lost in combat were never taken out by German tanks but by 8.8cm FlaK, 10.5cm leFH and several by AT mines].

2) The British had 308 tanks in France on 10th May 1940 and 284 additional ones were sent during the Battle of France = 592 tanks. In Abbeville and Arras alone the British lost 167 of their tanks. Several other British tanks were lost around Boulogne and Rouen but most of the remaining tanks were simply abandoned or lost due to mechanical breakdowns and could not be recovered and repaired in front of the advancing German troops.

3) Belgium had 50 light tanks and 228 tank destroyers but no data about the actual losses. However they were only used in very small groups and were probably all lost or abandoned.

4) Germany had 2,636 German tanks on 10th May 1940. 288 additional tanks were received during the 1940 campaign for a total of 2,924 tanks. According to Thomas Jentz, 839 German tanks are completely destroyed during May-June 1940. Beside these tanks we must list the 99 Panzerjäger I and 24 StuG IIIs but I have no information about their losses.

French tanks Captured

In their book, Regenberg & Sheibert mention the capture of 500 Renault FT17, 800 Renault R35/39/40, 600 Hotchkiss H35/39, 50 FCM36, 60 Renault B1bis and 300 Somua S35 wrecks after the campaign (numbers are probably not the 100% exact ones).

On 7th July 1940, general Halder writes that it is unlikely to re-use rapidly these booties and end August 1940 indeed only 33 French tanks are repaired/operational.

On 5th November 1941 the number available after repair had increased rapidly and includes 500 Renault FT17, 125 Renault R35, 200 Hotchkiss, 20 Somua etc. There is an appendix discussing from that in "1940 - L'effondrement" by Henri de Wailly. There were also Panhard 178 recovered and significant numbers of Lorraine 37L tractors, including new ones apparently.

For the Renault Renault FT17, it should be noted that the Germans seized large numbers of FT17 tanks which were stored and disarmed in tank parks. For example in Gien, there was a big park with about 1,000 "wrecks" of FT17 tanks : generally out of use, generally without turret and without armament. No doubt that many hulls or other pieces from these abandoned tanks stored in a park were also used by the Germans. But these 1,000 tanks where not in service with the French army.

Panzerkampfwagen 35R 731(f) (Renault R35) types

- Panzerkampfwagen 35R 731(f)
- Befehlspanzer 35R (f) (26 produced)
- Munitionspanzer 35R 731(f)
- Bergeschlepper 35R 731(f) (towing of vehicles)
- Zugkraftwagen 35R 731(f)
- 4.7cm Pak(t) auf PzKpfw 35R (f) (200 produced)
- 5cm Pak38 auf PzKpfw 35R (f)
- Flammenwerferpanzer 35R (f)
- Mörserzugmittel 35R (f) (Artillerie-Schlepper)
- some were used in armored trains

Training for Operation Seelöwe, Sea Lion

French Vehicles in Normandy 1944

100. Panzer Abteilung (committed to 91. ID)
Panzerkampfwagen 35R 731(f)
Panzerkampfwagen 39H 735(f)
Panzerkampfwagen 35S 739(f)
Flammenwerferpanzer Renault B2 (f)
Panzerkampfwagen 17R 730c(f)
4,7cm Pak(t) auf PzKpfw 35R (f)

4.7 cm Pak(t) (Sfl) auf Fgst.Pz.Kpfw.35 R 731(f) in Normandy, 1942

The tank destroyers never returned to the Eastern Front. This didn't mean that the 4.7 cm Pak(t) (Sfl) auf Fgst.Pz.Kpfw.35 R 731(f)'s service was over. Conditions in France allowed the questionable vehicle to keep serving. Film footage shows the trips of these tank destroyers along the beaches of Normandy. The conditions here weren't ideal, but they were far removed from a frozen crew hopelessly trying to bring their picky vehicle back to life.

As of June of 1943, forces stationed in France had 96 4.7 cm Pak(t) (Sfl) auf Fgst.Pz.Kpfw.35 R 731(f), 85 of these were in working order. The largest amount (24) was in the 319th Infantry Division that was occupying Guernsey and Jersey. Several of these tank destroyers were scattered among 15 infantry divisions. 3 were in the 100th Tank Regiment, 6 were sent to the

657th anti-tank battalion. By December of 1943, the overall number of 4.7 cm Pak(t) (Sfl) auf Fgst.Pz.Kpfw.35 R 731(f) was reduced to 92, but the number of functional vehicles was 88.

Panzer 35R(f) with a former Austrian M35 armoured car, a Steyr ADGZ armoured car (52 built)

A significant amount of 4.7 cm Pak(t) (Sfl) auf Fgst.Pz.Kpfw.35 R 731(f) remained in French Wehrmacht units in June of 1944. Despite the slow speed of these obsolete tank destroyers, they still had some fight left in them. Potentially, they could knock out any Allied tank with the exception of the Churchill, but their success was much more humble in reality. They were unable to influence the course of battle in any serious way. Nevertheless, one of the last recorded instances of the 4.7 cm Pak(t) (Sfl) auf Fgst.Pz.Kpfw.35 R 731(f) in combat was in the fall of 1944. 2 Tank destroyers from the 712th Infantry Division took part in battle.

Knocked out 4.7 cm Pak(t) (Sfl) auf Fgst.Pz.Kpfw.35 R 731(f) and Panzerkampfwagen 35R 731(f). Most likely, these vehicles are from the 100th Tank Regiment that fought for Cherbourg

Panzerkampfwagen 35R 731(f) (Renault R35)

Panzerkampfwagen 35R 731(f)

Other designation: Renault R35
Type: Captured light tank
Manufacturer: Renault Captured from French Army in 1940
Crew: 2
Weight (tons): 10
Length: 4.02m
Width: 1.87m
Height: 1.94m
Engine: Renault 4cyl 5.8L, 80hp at 2.200rpm
Gearbox: 4 forward. I reverse Speed (km/h): 20
Range (km): 140
Radio: FuGS
Armament: One 3.7cm KwK18(1) L/21, One 7.5mm MG31(1), Ammunition: 58. 2.400 MG rounds
Traverse: 360 (hand)

The Renault R35 was the main infantry tank of the French Amy, and was issued to the independent tank battalions which supported the infantry divisions. First ordered in January 1935, there were 870 available in May 1940 Despite heavy losses a considerable number were captured intact. They were modified to German requirements, and a number were issued to troops operating in secondary theatres or against partisans. A considerable number had their turrets removed and were issued as Artillerie Schlepper or Munitionsschlepper 35R(f) Their other main use was as the basis of a self-propelled anti-tank gun, and some were exported to Italy in 1941.

Specific features: The tanks issued to German units had the turret observation dome removed and replaced by an opening hatch A radio set was fitted with its aerial mounted on the front left-hand mudguard.

In combat service the Pz Kpfw 35R were issued to only one regular unit of the Panzer troops. the reforming 100th Panzerbrigade of the 21st Panzer Division (New). in 1943. These returned to the depot after a few months. Six platoons of 35R were sent to the Channel Islands in 1941 and. also in 1941, twenty-six 35R were issued as Command-vehicles to the Panzerjaeger detachments equipped with 4.7cm Pak (1) auf Pz Kpfw 35R (f). A number of other 35R were scattered among infantry divisions garrisoned in France.

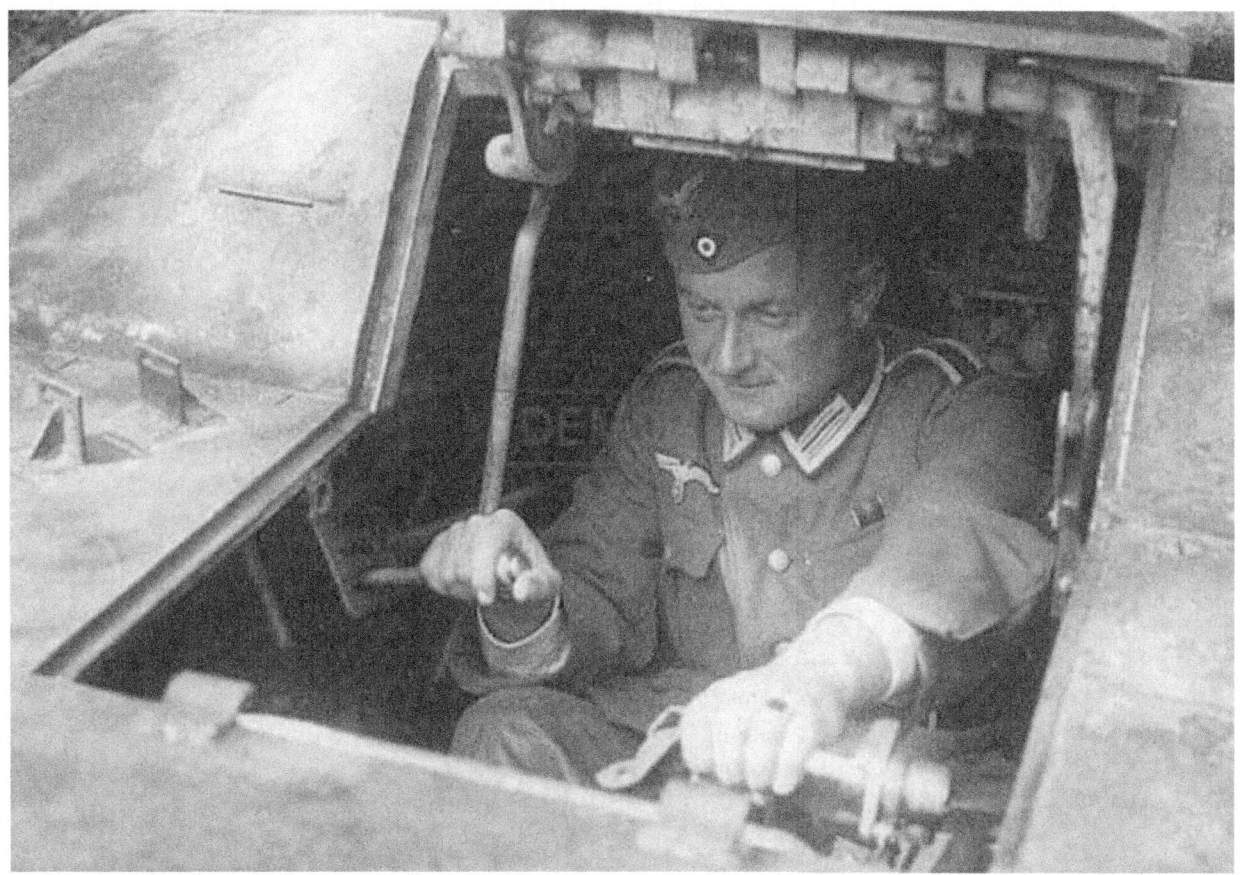

A view of the driver compartment, and handling bars

The tanks have been painted over with a darker paint and Balkenkreuz added on the turret and the front of the hull but no other modification seemed to have been done: no radio added and the original cupola has not been replaced

Renault 35R and a Peugout DK5 or 402 Camionette. The R 35 on the left seems to still carry the French registration number in the front and the French camouflage paint. The tanks on the right (and on the 1st picture) have been painted over with a darker paint and Balkenkreuz added on the turret and the front of the hull but no other modification seemed to have been done: no radio added and the original cupola has not been replaced.

The French markings and the shutters indicate that the picture was taken in France. The short roof overhang and the small windows on the left of the building could indicate a sunny location, possibly south of the Loire river but no other indication to figure out a more precise location

Renault-R35 towing a Lorraine tractor

Captured Renault R35. It's put straight into the fight against its previous owners. The markings are not formalized

Renault R35, used directly by front line troops in France 1940

Renault R35 731 (f)'s, showing commanders hatch

Renault R35 pressed into Wehrmacht use,. picture from May 1940

Renault 35R(f) used for drivers training

Panzerkampfwagen 35R 731(f) taken from the German Order Police. Note German aerial mast

A beute Renault R35, on the left a Belgian T13 early version and in the back of the picture a dummy Schulungspanzer on a Opel P4(Schulungspanzer - School tank)

Renault 35R(f) beute platoon, Zug in German

Befehlspanzer 35R (f) (26 produced)

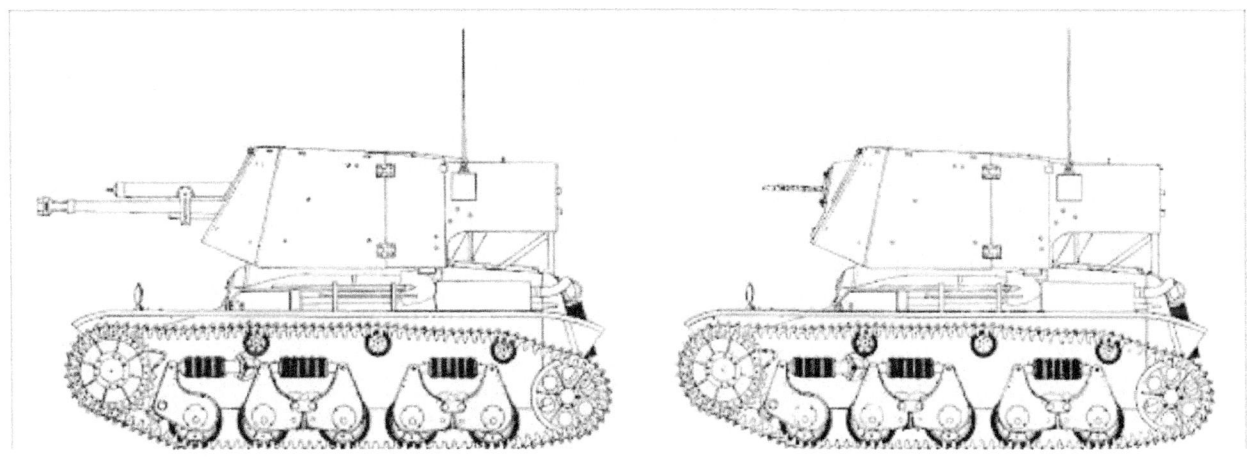

Column of Befehlspanzer auf 35R(f) für 4.7cm PaK(t)(Command tank for Anti-tank guns) and 4.7cm PaK(t) auf 35R(f)

Befehlswagen für 4,7cm-Pak(t)-Einheiten auf PzKpfw 35R(f) on the Eastern Front. Must be in winter 1941/42. These command vehicles where armed with a MG34. According to Spielberger only 26 were build

Munitionspanzer 35R 731(f)

A certain number of the Renault 25R were transformed into Munitionsschlepper by simple removal of the turret. The turrets were installed on blockhouses of the Atlantic Wall or assigned to the defense of important sites.

A STZ-5 soviet artillery tractor in the background with a Munitionspanzer 35R(f) in front

A Renault R40 rebuilt as a Munition carrier

Bergeschlepper 35R 731(f) (towing of vehicles)

The Bergeschlepper were turret-less and unarmed, though some were fitted with a small shield for an MG34.

Bergeschlepper 35R (f) at work. The crew added a windshield that made it much more comfortable to drive

Another result of a conversion by removing the turret and ammunition racks, was the Bergeschlepper 35R (f) Armoured Recovert Vehicle. It was practically identical to the artillery tractor version aside from its tasks. Some of the most resourceful crews made further enhancements to the vehicle, for example by installing windshields or machinegun mounts. Approximately 90 such vehicles were made.

Zugkraftwagen 35R 731(f)

The Artillerie Schlepper/Munitionsschlepper were turret- less and unarmed, though some were fitted with a small shield for an MG34.

Renault R35 in German service without it's original turret. Instead a field modification turret of welded armor plates with a machine gun. 27. maj 1942

Umbau von Panzerkampfwagen 35R(f) on the eastern front, 1941

Umbau von Panzerkampfwagen 35R (f) on the eastern front, 1941

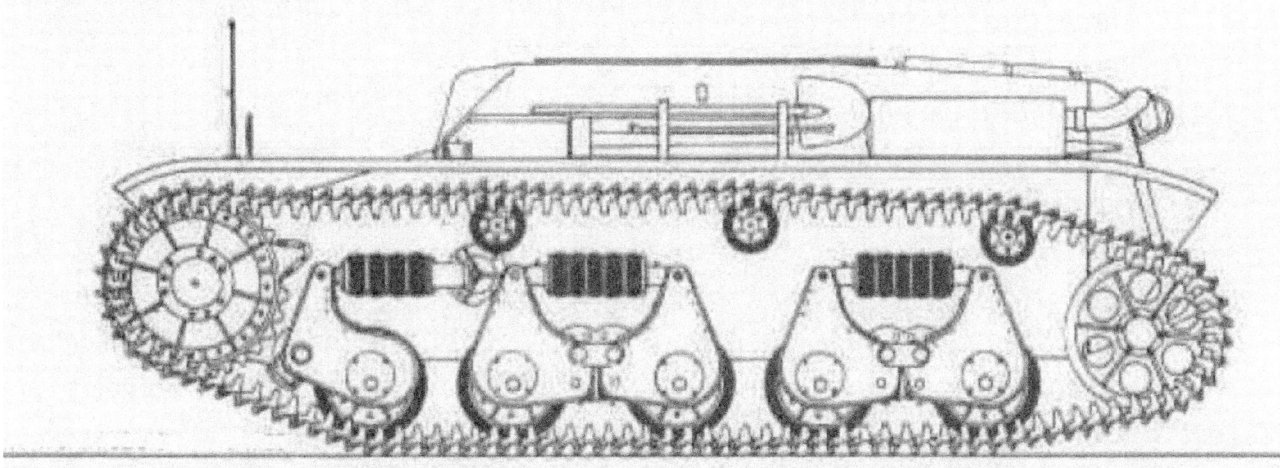

Detailed drawing of the 35R Zugkraftwagen

4.7cm Pak(t) auf PzKpfw 35R (f) (200 produced)

Type: Self-propelled anti-tank gun on captured tank captured tank chassis
Manufacturer: Alkett, Altmärkische Kettenwerk GmbH, (Altmark track works)
174 converted from May 1941 to October 1941
Crew: 3
Engine: Renault 4cyl 5.8lit 80hp at 2,200rpm
Weight (tons): 10.5
Gearbox: 4 forward, 1 reverse
Length: 4.3m
Speed (km/hr): 19
Width: 1.87m
Height: 2.11m
Range (km): 140
Radio: FuG Spr d
Armament: One 4.7cm Pak (1) L/43.4
Traverse: 17 left 171 right (hand)
Elevation: -8° 12°
Sight: ZF2 x 30

On 25 December 1940 the Renault R35 was ordered replace the Pz Kpfw I as the chassis to carry the 4.7cm PaK when the conversion of those vehicles would cease in February 1 Like the Pz Kpfw 1. the R35 was a two-man tank of limited fighting potential. A mild steel prototype was delivered on 8 February 1941. The firm ordered to this was Alkett. It was founded in 1937 as a subsidiary of Rheinmetall-Borsig AG, which in turn was a subsidiary of the government-controlled Reichswerke Hermann Göring. The main facility was sited on the Rota-wagon and Maschinenbau GmbH plants, which had not been in use since 1928.

Alkett was the company that Major Alfred Becker worked with, initially in early 1942 to help create self-propelled artillery pieces by use of captured French Lorraine Schlepper ammunition carriers. Becker converted these vehicles to carry the 150 mm sFH 18. Becker's later work converting captured French vehicles to carry German weapons was assisted by Alkett, which produced the steel superstructures for the vehicles Becker was modifying in France.

The first order of Renault Panzerjägers was for 130 units, but this was continued in July 1941 by a further 70. This was Germany's second Panzerjäger (Sf) and the protection was improved over and above the Panzerjäger I, by having a fully-enclosed, but open-topped superstructure. 26 Pz Kpfw 35R were issued as to be converted to Command vehicles alongside the Selbstfahrlafette(Self-propelled).

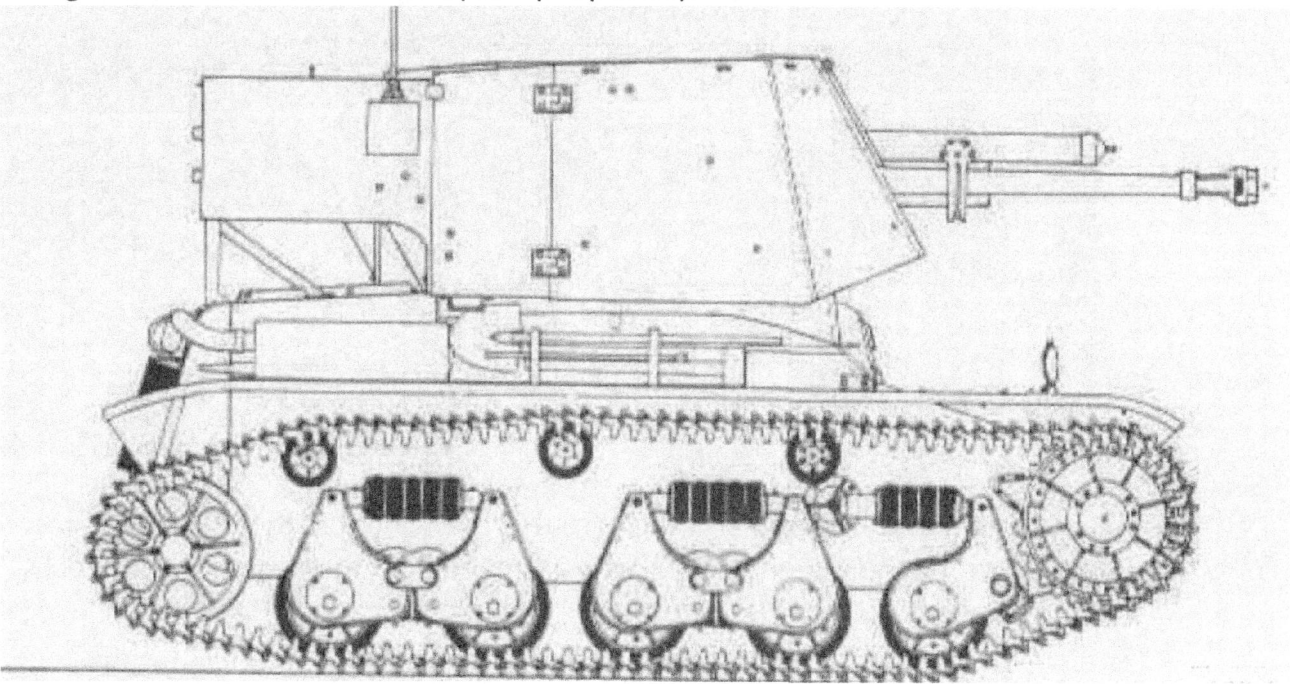

It had some specific features like a Large open-topped fixed superstructure replaced the turret, and storage space was increased by extending this over the engine compartment. The Germans had in their inventory a number of the more potent Czechoslovakian 47 mm Kanon P.U.V.vz.38 anti-tank guns, known as the 4.7 cm Panzerabwehrkanone 36(t), or simply as 4.7 cm PaK(t). Due to its better firepower, the Germans decided to use this cannon to arm the first self-propelled anti-tank vehicle, known simply as the Panzerjäger I. Essentially a Panzer I chassis which the turret was replaced with a 4.7 cm PaK(t) mount and a three-sided shield. While this concept proved to have merit, as shown in France, it was far from perfect. The chassis of the 35R was insufficient for the task and it was poorly protected.

Panzerjäger I (Tank hunter I)or its formal name 4.7 cm PaK(t) (Sf) auf Panzerkampfwagen I ohne Turm (translating to 4.7 cm antitank gun (Czech) (self-propelled) on turretless Pz.Kpfw. I)

The tank destroyer variant of the Renault was shown to Adolf Hitler on March 31st, 1941, and he approved of the modernization The first 30 vehicles were built in March of 1941, and their numbers grew to 93 by May. Another 33 were built in June, 5 in July, 22 in August, 28 in September, and 19 in October.

On February 27th, 1941, it was decided to arm the 559th and 561st anti-tank battalions, which was equipped with 3.7cm Pak 36 towed guns, with the 4.7 cm Pak(t) (Sfl) auf Fgst.Pz.Kpfw.35 R 731(f). Later, the 661st anti-tank battalion was re-armed as well. By the start of Operation Barbarossa, the 559th battalion was a part of Army Group North and the 561th and 611th battalions in Army Group Center.

Each of these battalions consisted of an HQ unit and three Kompanie (Companies). Each Company was divided into smaller three-vehicle strong Zuge (Platoons). There was an additional Company sent to the 43rd Battalion, supplied with a few vehicles, to act as a reserve and training unit. The remaining vehicles would be mainly distributed in smaller numbers to various Infantry Divisions.

A total of 174 4.7cm Pak auf Pz Kpfw 35R and 26 command vehicles were issued to the Panzerjäger abteillungen stationed in secondary theatres. By May 1942. 183 were in service. the remainder having been re-converted to Artillerie Schlepper. At the start of 1944, 110 units were in service, mainly in France, with a few in the occupied Channel Islands.

4.7cm PaK(t) auf Reanult 35R(f) on a Sd. Anh 115 trailer. To reduce the wear and tear on the suspension and engine, the Germans often employed trailers to transport their tanks

4.7cm PaK(t) on PzKpfw 35R(f)

Renault R35 Panzerjäger

Armament

The gun used to arm this vehicle was the captured Škoda 47 mm Kanon P.U.V.vz.38, known as the 4.7cm Panzerabwehrkanone 36(t), or simply the 4.7cm PaK(t) in German service. The standard armor-piercing Panzergranate 36(t) had a muzzle velocity of 775 m/s and a maximum effective range of 1.5 km. The armor penetration of this round was 48-59 mm at 500 m and 41 mm at 1000m.

Škoda 47 mm Kanon P.U.V.vz.38, paraded with mortars

In order to extend its operational effectiveness, a new Panzer granate Patr.40 tungsten round was developed (the muzzle velocity was 1080 m/s). The Germans lacked sufficient tungsten, so this type of ammunition could not be produced in large quantities and its usage was rare. The 4.7cm PaK(t) also fired high-explosive rounds (2.3 kg weight) with impact fuses to be used against light armor and infantry.

The gun itself, without the wheels and the trail legs, was simply bolted on the front, where the R35's turret ring was previously positioned. The 4.7 cm gun had an elevation of -8° to +12° and a traverse angle of 17.5° to the left and right side. The elevation and traverse were controlled by two handwheels located on the gun's left side. The main monocular gunsight was not changed. The total ammunition load is unknown. The smaller Panzerjäger I was able to carry 86 rounds, it would be logical to assume that the new Panzerjäger 35R's ammunition load would be similar, if not slightly larger.

For crew protection, one MP38/40 submachine gun was carried inside. The ammunition load for the submachine gun was 192 rounds. As the Panzerjäger was designed to cooperate with infantry, the lack of a machine gun was not considered an issue.

Note how the rear of the superstructure is built over the engine
compartment, and support tubes under the ammunition bin

Pictures seem to be from factory

4,7-cm-Pak(t) auf Panzerkampfwagen 35R(f)- ohne Turm

4,7-cm-Pak(t) auf Panzerkampfwagen 35R(f)- ohne Turm

The Panzerjäger had a crew of three, with the commander, who was also the gunner, the loader and the driver. The driver's position was on the left side of the vehicle. He entered his position through a two-part hatch with a visor. The other two crewmen were positioned in the new armored fighting compartment. The commander/gunner was positioned to the left of the gun, and the loader to the right of him. Who operated the radio is unclear.

4,7cm-Pak(t) auf PzKpfw 35R(f) in Mogilev

Panzerjäger 35R shared a number of positive and negative characteristics with its cousin, the Panzerjäger I. It provided the German infantry with a more mobile anti-tank platform with a relatively good gun and somewhat better protection than the earlier Panzerjäger I.

While it was slow, the infantry it was designed to provide cover for were themselves not a very mobile force, so this was not a major issue. It was also quicker to bring into action than the towed guns normally assigned to the infantry divisions.

The first available vehicles were used to form three 30 vehicle Panzerjäger Abteilung – Pz.Jg.Abt (self-propelled anti-tank battalions), the 559th, 561st, and the 611th. Each of these battalions consisted of an HQ unit and three Kompanie (Companies). Each Company was divided into smaller three-vehicle strong Zuge (Platoons). There was an additional Company sent to the 43rd Battalion, supplied with a few vehicles, to act as a reserve and training unit. The remaining vehicles would be mainly distributed in smaller numbers to various Infantry Divisions into there antitank units.

Interestingly the Panzerjäger I's was organized like this: (From Thomas Jentz's book Panzer Tracts No. 7-1: Panzerjäger, page 7-46);
The following organiztion is for a non-divisional anti-tank battalion.

1 x Stab Pz.Jg.Abt. (Kstn 1106) with 1 x Pz.Kpfw.1b (SdKfz.101).
1 x Nachr.Zug Pz.Jg.Abt. (Kstn 1192).
3 x Pz.Jg.Kp. (mot. S) (Kstn 1148 dated Apr. 2, 1940) with 4.7 cm Pak (t) (auf Sfl.) and munitions-sonder-Anhaenger 32.
Each Panzerjäger kompanie had 9 Panzerjäger I's for a battalion total of 27 vehicles. With an Panzer I as its Kompagni befehlswagen.

Camouflaged Panzerjäger I's

The problem with this vehicle was its mechanical unsuitability for the Eastern Front (a problem that most French vehicles had when they were used there by the Germans). As a vehicle it was at its best, when it stayed on good roads.

Poor roads and cold climate prevented the Panzerjäger 35R from being of any use on the Eastern front. The armor protection, especially the all around (but open-top) crew compartment, was still weak by the standards of 1942. In any case, the Panzerjäger 35R was surely a good way of increasing the effectiveness of the obsolete R35 tank, but was let down by its basis.

The Panzerjäger 35Rs, like many other German captured armored vehicles, were mobilized for the invasion of the Soviet Union in June 1941. The 559th Abteilung was allocated to Army Group North, while the 561st and 611th Abteilung was allocated to Army Group Center. For these vehicles, Operation Barbarossa started badly. Almost all there vehicles were out of action due to mechanical breakdowns just a few days after the start of the German attack. For example, with the 611th Battalion, it lost all its vehicles on the first day of the attack. In desperation, the unit was instead equipped with the 3.7 cm PaK 36 towed gun and some Soviet captured anti-tank guns. The 559th Battalion also had the same fate, replacing its vehicles with 3.7 cm PaK anti-tank guns. The 561st was pulled back from the front, temporarily waiting to replace the tank destroyers with towed anti-tank guns.

Another unit that was sent to the Soviet Union, late 1941, was the 318th Company, which had ten 35R Panzerjägers and 2 command vehicles. These performed poorly based on the units report dated from February 1942. In this report, it was noted that these vehicles had poor engines, which were ill suited for the conditions of the Eastern front. Bad weather and the poor road system prevented long road marches with this vehicle. Due to the low temperatures, the engines could not be started and even the road wheels would be blocked and unable to move because of the low temperatures. After the poor performance, no more 35R anti-tank vehicles would be sent to the East. Some of these vehicles was allocated to allies, like the Hungarians.

5cm Pak38 auf PzKpfw 35R (f)

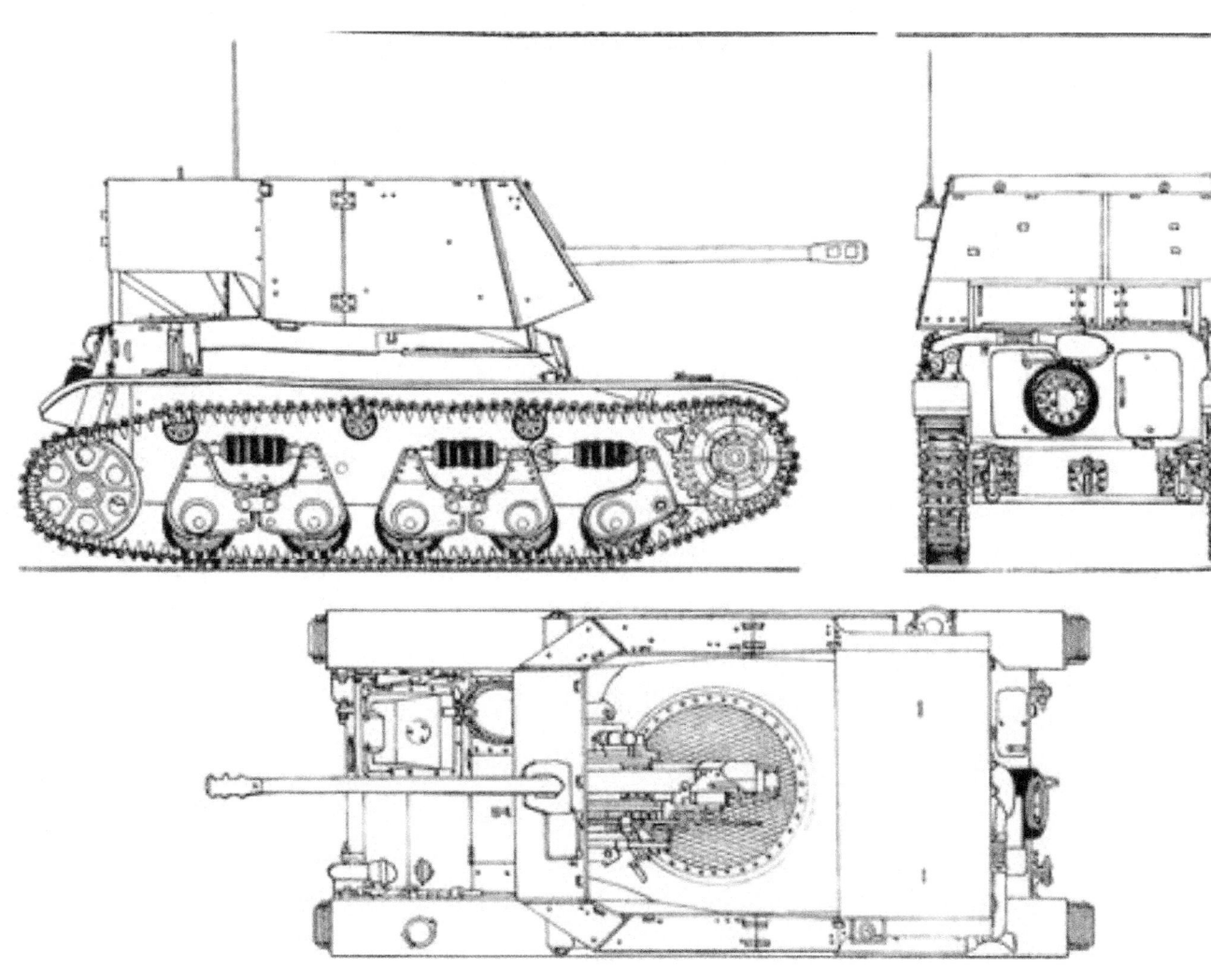

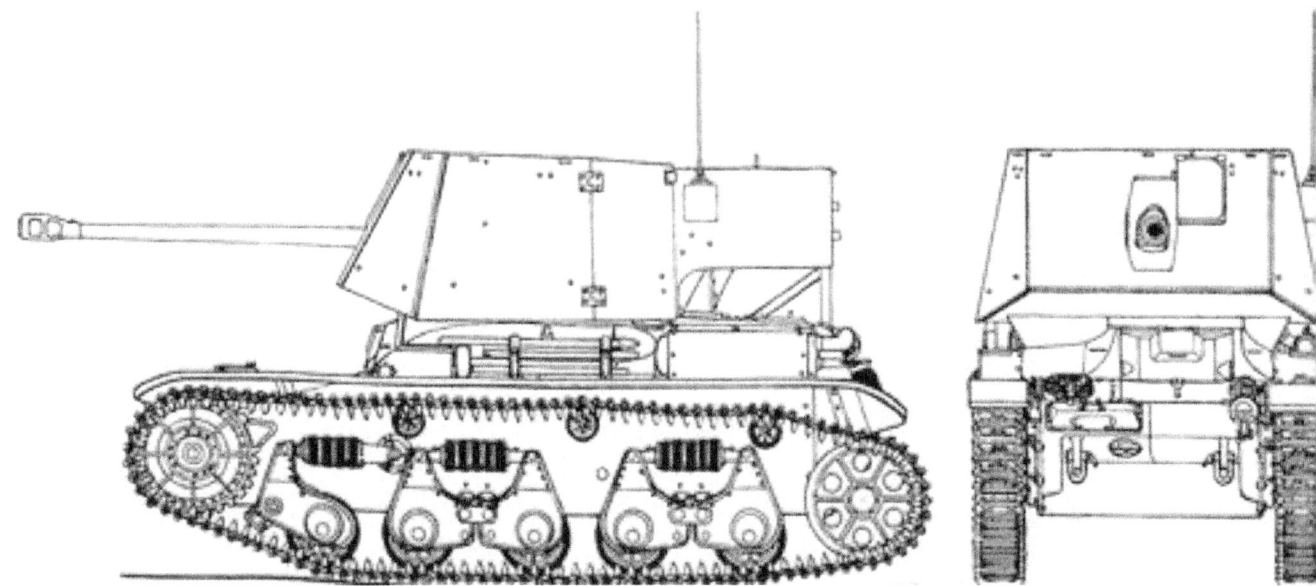

At the end of July 1941, Alkett was instructed by Wa Prüf 6(this was the Waffen Prüf 6, which was the weapons department for design of Tanks and motorized equipment)to design and produce a modified version of the Panzerkampfwagen 35R armed with the 5cm PaK 38. This vehicle was designated 5cm PaK 38 auf 35R(f). Once adopted, it was to be allocated to anti-tank units of standard Infantry Divisions. Due to the addition of the larger gun, the weight of the vehicle rose to 11.5 tonnes. While one vehicle was to be ready by August 1941, it is unlikely that this was ever built.

The 5cm gun was a more powerful weapon with much stronger recoil, and it is not clear if the R35 chassis could have successfully handled it without major mechanical problems. The poor performance of this chassis and its suspension probably also influenced the decision to drop this project.

Flammenwerferpanzer 35R (f)

There is some doubt as to this version. Some sources lists it. In any case there are some pictures of it.
It was a Panzerkampfwagen 35R 731(f) (Renault R35) conversion, identical to the 4.7cm Pak(t) auf PzKpfw 35R (f) but armed with a Flammenwerfer and called Flammenwerferpanzer 35R (f). Only few made.

Panzerkampfwagen 35R 731(f) (Renault R35) conversion, identical to the 4.7cm Pak(t) auf PzKpfw 35R (f) but armed with a Flammenwerfer and called Flammenwerferpanzer 35R (f)

Mörserzugmittel 35R (f) (Artillerie-Schlepper)

The Artillerie Schlepper/Munitionsschlepper were turret- less and unarmed, though some were fitted with a small shield for an MG34.

Some of the captured R35s did make it to the eastern front, but not as tanks. Their turrets and ammunition racks were removed and suddenly the Germans had a new makeshift artillery tractor. 110 of these vehicles (some called it Umbau von Panzerkampfwagen 35R(f)(meaning rebuild R35)) were sent to artillery battery units that operated the sFH 18 howitzers and the heavier 17cm K 18/21cm Mrs 18 cannons in February 1941. They were used successfully and by the March of 1942, Wehrmacht still had 52 of these tractors in active service. Considering that the developers never envisaged the R35 being used as a tractor and that these loads it hauled around was very heavy. Their use was a very good result of an obsolete vehicle, praticly unsuitable for the eastern front.

Mörserzugmittel 35R (f) (Artillerie-Schlepper) mit 21cm mortar

Renault R35 Morserzugmittel on a train to the Eastern Front

Renault 35R Morser schlepper. A second one can be seen in the back

Same unit as above. Renault 35R Morser schlepper. A second one can be seen in the back

Mörserzugmittel 35R (f) (Artillerie-Schlepper) mit 21cm mortar

35 R (f) morserzugmittel towing a 21cm mortar

Umbau von Panzerkampfwagen Renault35R(f), morserzugmittel towing a 21cm mortar

Modifications

The Renault R35 was also used as a crane vehicles of several types only this photo below.

Renault R35 with a crane mounted on it, It seems to be a lengthened R35 chassis but it is not clear at all if it was a French test or modification, a vehicle produced for civilian tasks or maybe a later German modification

Renault 35R(f) modified with 3.7cm PaK36

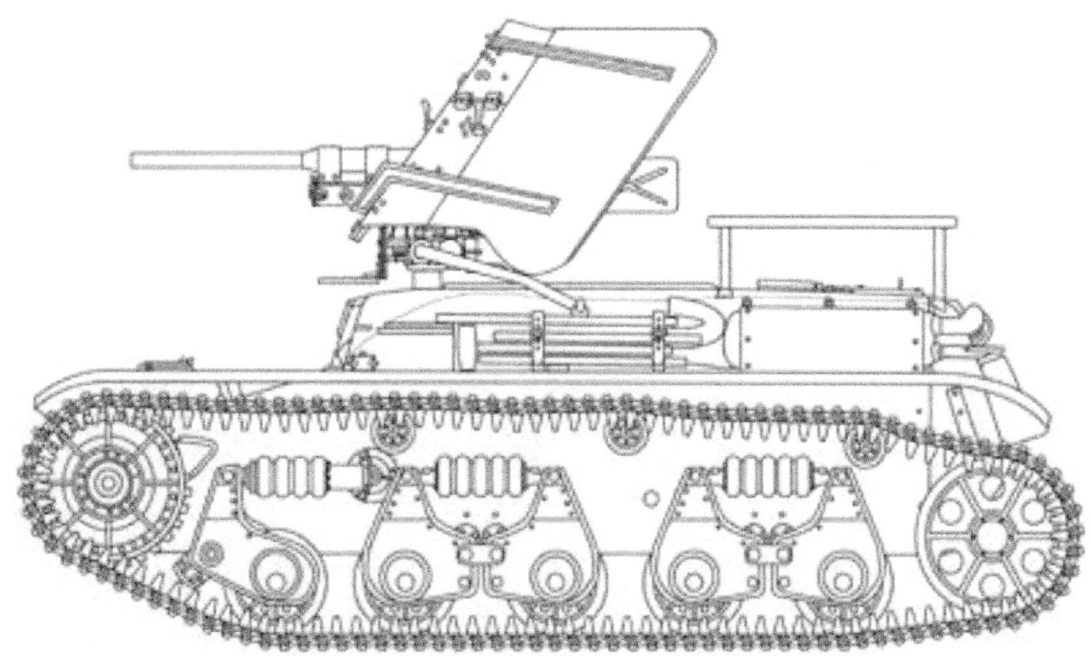

Drawing of 35R(f) modified with a 3.7cm PaK36, the 3.7cm was practicly of no use. unless on point blank range against the Soviet KV-1 or T-34

Renault 35R with a Soviet T-26 turret. Most likely this is a forward artillery observer vehicle with a fixed turret. The shoulder straps of the turrets of the T-26. and R35 are different.

Renault 35R with a Soviet T-26 turret

Some claims the photos of the R35 with a T-26 turret is fake. The turret ring diameter of the T-26 turret was 20cm bigger than the one for the APX R turret and it was practically impossible to make such a conversion in field conditions if the turret should turn. There are other suggestions that the Turret might be in a fixed position.

The turrets of the vehicles that were converted to ARVs and tractors were used as well – they travelled west and were used as fixed fortifications of the Atlantic Wall.

End of the line

In the west, the fate of the captured R35s was different. The tanks there were continued to be used as training vehicles, even though the Germans preferred to use the Hotchkiss H39 because it was somewhat more mobile. Apart from that, three dozen Panzerkampfwagen 35R 731(f) vehicles were given to Waffen SS by the end of 1941. These were used in the Balkans. On 1.3.1943, 50 captured R35s were still attached to the 100th Panzer Regiment. By the end of May 1943, 46 were still attached to the 100th Panzer Brigade, 8 to the 711th Infantry Division. The 712th and 708th Infantry Divisions had two each and 22 more were attached to the 12th Special Operations Panzer Company.

These captured vehicles actively fought during the Normandy campaign. The 100th Panzer Regiment fought the Americans in the Cherbourg region (with quite predictable results). 2 of these tanks belonged to the 206th Panzer Regiment HQ unit, also fighting around Cherbourg. And finally, a number of the R35s and R40s fought in Paris as a part of the "Paris Panzer Company". These were destroyed during the August 1944 liberation of the city, some were knocked out by the French 2nd Armored Division of General Leclerc. Some were even captured by the French Resistance fighters and used against Germans.

Appendix

The organization of the Wehrmachts weapons department, was divide into the following

Wa Prüf 1 - Ammunition
Wa Prüf 2 - Infantry
Wa Prüf 3 - Chefkonstrukteur
Wa Prüf 4 - Artillery
Wa Prüf 5 - Engineering and railway
Wa Prüf 6 - Tanks and motorized equipment
Wa Prüf 7 - Signal
Wa Prüf 8 - Optical, survey, meteorological, artillery fire control, map-printing
Wa Prüf 9 - Gas protection(chemical)
Wa Prüf 10 - Anti-air
Wa Prüf 11 - Special equipment
Wa Prüf 12 - Proving grounds
Wa Prüf Fest - Fortress engineering

Literature

Pascal Danjou, 2005, Renault R35/R40, Editions du Barbotin, Ballainvilliers
T. L. Jentz and H.L. Doyle (2004) Panzer Tracts No7.1, Panzerjager.

Major J. Bingham (1973) French Infantry Tanks: Part II, AFV weapons
H. F. Duske, Panzerjager I, Nuts and Bolts

François Vauvillier, 2006, "Toute la Lumière sur le Canon de 37 SA 38",
Histoire de Guerre, Blindés et Matériel, N°74

W.J. Spielberger (1992) Beute-Kraftfahrzeuge und Panzer der Deutschen
Wehrmacht, Militärfahrzeuge.

White, B.T (1983). Tanks and other Armoured Fighting Vehicles of World War
II. Peerage books. ISBN 0-907408-35-4

D. Nešić, (2008), Naoružanje Drugog Svetskog Rata-Francuska, Beograd.

P. Chamberlain and H. Doyle (1978) Encyclopedia of German Tanks of World
War Two – Revised Edition, Arms and Armor press.

D. Doyle (2005). German military Vehicles, Krause Publications.

A. Lüdeke (2007) Waffentechnik im Zweiten Weltkrieg, Parragon Books.

S. Zaloga (2011) Armored attack 1944 U.S. Army tank combat in the
European theater from D-day to the Battle of the Bulge, Stackpole Books.

S.J. Zaloga (2014) French tanks of World War II (1), Osprey Publishing

Mahé, Yann (February 2011). "Le Blindorama : La Turquie, 1935 - 1945".
Batailles & Blindés (in French). No. 41. Caraktère

Printed in Great Britain
by Amazon

25529989R00044